Children's History of the World

THE MODERN WORLD

OXFORD
Children's History of the World

THE
MODERN
WORLD

Neil Grant

OXFORD
UNIVERSITY PRESS

OXFORD
UNIVERSITY PRESS

Oxford University Press is a department of the University of Oxford.
It furthers the University's objective of excellence in research, scholarship,
and education by publishing worldwide in

Oxford New York

Athens Auckland Bangkok Bogotá Buenos Aires Kolkata
Cape Town Chennai Dar es Salaam Delhi Florence Hong Kong Istanbul
Karachi Kuala Lumpur Madrid Melbourne Mexico City Mumbai
Nairobi Paris São Paulo Shanghai Singapore Taipei Tokyo Toronto Warsaw

with associated companies in Berlin Ibadan

Oxford is a registered trade mark of Oxford University Press
in the UK and in certain other countries

First published 2001
Some material in this book was previously
published in Children's History of the World 2000

British Library Cataloguing in Publication Data available

Paperback ISBN 0-19-910825-0

1 3 5 7 9 10 8 6 4 2

Printed in Malaysia

CONSULTANTS
Mike Corbishley
Dr. Narayani Gupta
Dr. Rick Halpern
Dr. Douglas H. Johnson
Rosemary Kelly
James Mason

Contents

How to use this book

This book is divided into double-page spreads, each on a different subject. At the end of the book there is a Timeline. This shows at a glance the developments in different regions of the world during the period covered by the section. There is also a Who's Who page, which gives short biographies of the most important people of the period, a Glossary of important words, and an Index.

Dates here show the time in history when the events took place.

The title describes the subject of the spread, like a newspaper headline.

The first paragraph sets the scene, explaining what the spread is about and why it is important.

Photographs and illustrations show paintings, objects, places, people and scenes from the past.

The American Civil War

The American Civil War began when the Southern states tried to leave the Union, which the federal government refused to accept. The defeat of the South, after four years of fighting and one million deaths, resulted in the end of slavery and a stronger union under Northern control.

North vs. South

The union of American states had been created to fight the British, and was never strong. The sharpest division was between the farming South, which depended on cotton produced by slaves, and the industrial North, where slavery was illegal. Some Northerners believed slavery should be abolished in the South too. The different views on slavery caused serious conflict as the country expanded westward. In the new territory of Kansas, fighting broke out between supporters and opponents of slavery. In politics, tempers were high. The Democratic Party, which depended on support in North and South, split in two, for and against slavery, each with its own candidate for president. As a result, the 1860 election was won by Abraham Lincoln, candidate of the Republicans, a new party of Northerners which was strongly against slavery in the South.

Many Southerners believed that the Republicans would end slavery, taking away their workforce, and feared the blacks would attack them. Before Lincoln had entered the White House, the Southern states officially withdrew from the Union and founded the Confederate States of America. When the Confederates attacked a federal fort at Fort Sumter, South Carolina, in April 1861, the Civil War began.

△ The Northern (Union) and Southern (Confederate) states. The war was important for other countries too. For example, most of the cotton used in European factories came from the South. When the war stopped cotton imports, thousands of workers lost their jobs.

Confederate States
Union States
territories not yet states

War

The Union had big advantages over the Confederates: more men, more money, most of the industry and railways. They also had control of the navy, which prevented the Confederates getting help from abroad. But the Confederates had great fighting spirit and, at first, better generals. Besides, they only had to defend the South, while the Union had to invade and conquer it. As a result, the war lasted four years, before the Confederates were forced to surrender.

◁ Although the Confederacy had no navy, it had two or three warships. Most famous was the *Alabama*, a sailing ship with a steam engine. Her career lasted two years, and she captured or destroyed about 70 Union merchant ships. In June 1864 she fought her final duel with a Union frigate in the English Channel, and was sunk.

◁ At the Battle of Chattanooga in November 1863, Union forces led by General Grant defeated the Confederates in a decisive confrontation. The Union could now use Chattanooga, in Tennesee, as a base for General Sherman's invasion of Georgia.

1861 - 1865

Events of the Civil War

1861 February: Jefferson Davis is elected president of the Confederacy.
April: Confederates attack Fort Sumter.
July: Confederate victory at Bull Run.
1862 August: Confederates under General Lee invade the North.
October: Lee's advance is checked.
1863 January: Lincoln proclaims the freedom of slaves.
July: Union victory at Gettysburg.
November: Lincoln delivers his Gettysburg Address in praise of unity and democracy.
1864 Union army under Sherman invades Georgia and burns Atlanta.
1865 Confederate commander Robert E. Lee surrenders to General Ulysses S. Grant at Appomatox.

The end of slavery

Some slaves escaped to the North, some were Union spies, and some joined the army. In 1862 President Lincoln's Emancipation Proclamation declared an end to slavery, causing celebrations among the slaves (below). About 4 million slaves became legally free, but they had no money and no property, and still depended on their former owners. Even in many northern states, blacks were not allowed to vote in elections until after 1870. A long struggle for equality lay ahead.

26

27

The text is divided into short blocks, each with its own heading. They describe one part of the main subject of the spread.

Captions describe the illustrations and how they relate to the main text.

Fact boxes list key events associated with the subject.

Coloured boxes give more details about major events or important people linked to the subject.

Many pages also have a map, to show the country or region where the events took place.

Introduction

One reason for studying history is to learn how the world turned out the way it is now. This book is about what happened in little more than 100 years of history, during the last part of the 18th century and the 19th century. A century is not a long time in history, but between 1775 and 1900 the world changed more than ever before.

The most important change began in the West (Europe and countries ruled by people of European descent). It was really a series of changes connected with the way goods are produced, when huge factories replaced cottage workshops. That in turn changed the way people lived and worked. At first these changes affected only Western countries, but in the end they spread to other regions. They are grouped together under the name of the Industrial Revolution.

Other kinds of revolution were almost as important for the future. In 1776 the USA declared its independence and ended British rule. By 1900 it was one of the three richest countries in the world – and still growing fast.

Soon after the Americans founded their democratic republic, the French Revolution broke out. France became a republic in which everyone was equal according to law. The revolution ended with the rule of Napoleon, a great general who conquered much of Europe and made himself an emperor. But other revolutions and demands for reform followed, and in time the ideas of the French Revolution were successful. By 1900 most European countries were on the way to freedom, equal rights and democracy.

The Industrial Revolution increased the power and wealth of the West. In 1800, countries such as France and Great Britain already ruled colonies abroad. European empires steadily increased. British colonies were founded in Australia and New Zealand. The British also became the rulers of India. Parts of Asia and most of Africa fell under European rule. Even in countries not ruled by Europeans, Western power and money had a powerful effect. Western bankers and businessmen had some control over the government of China. Japan, however, followed the example of the West and quickly became the first great industrial power in Asia.

Europe itself was not only more prosperous but also more peaceful than in any earlier century. Middle-class Europeans in 1900 could feel satisfied with their way of life. But in the next century, peace would collapse in total war, and European world rule would end.

American Independence

In 1776 the British colonies in North America declared their independence from Great Britain. In the war that followed, the colonists defeated the British forces and joined together as the United States of America.

Revolution

After 1763, Britain tried to bring the colonies under closer control. When the British parliament imposed new taxes, the colonists objected because they had no representatives there. Anti-British feeling was strongest in Massachusetts, where British restrictions on trade hit hardest. After the Boston Tea Party of 1773 (below), the government punished Massachusetts with new penalties. Anger rose. Massachusetts was also the centre of revolutionary ideas. Tom Paine's *Common Sense* (1776) was eagerly read. He wanted a democratic republic, an end to slavery and equal rights for women. In Boston in 1775 revolutionaries were collecting guns. When British soldiers tried to seize them, shots were fired. The American Revolution had begun.

▷ A minuteman. The minutemen were groups of part-time soldiers, who fought against the British. They gained their name because they said they could be ready for action at a minute's notice.

▽ The Boston Tea Party. In a protest against the British East India Company's control of the tea trade, a gang of Bostonians, disguised as Mohawks (Native Americans), threw the Company's tea into the harbour in 1773.

War

Although the 13 colonies were very different, and many people there were loyal to Britain, the colonies agreed to have their own central government, and appointed George Washington as their army commander. The rebels were not trained soldiers, but they knew the country well, unlike the European soldiers. Most of them were also experienced hunters, and they had better guns. After a long, hard struggle the colonists, with valuable help from France, defeated Britain's professional armies, which included soldiers hired in Germany. The last British army was forced to surrender at Yorktown in 1781 when its supplies were blocked by the French fleet. Two years later, Great Britain reluctantly recognised the independent United States of America.

△ George Washington

The new nation

Representatives of the 13 colonies, which were now independent states, met to decide on a form of government for the new nation. After long discussions, they agreed on a constitution in 1787. It created a federation, with a federal (central) government, an elected president, and a congress (legislature) of representatives from each state. The federal government controlled national affairs, such as taxation, defence and foreign policy, but each state also had an elected local government to control its own affairs.

The United States of America became the first modern democracy, in which the power of the government depended on the agreement of the people. But who were the people? The constitution said that all people were equal, yet slaves remained slaves, with no rights. Native Americans were also ignored, and no women could vote. Even so, it was a great advance on other Western governments, which were still controlled by small groups of rich men.

The Declaration of Independence

The Declaration of Independence, of 4 July 1776, explained why the Continental Congress had voted for independence from Britain. It was mainly written by Thomas Jefferson, a future president. It claimed that 'all men are created equal' and have the right to 'Life, Liberty and the pursuit of Happiness'. Its main purpose was to persuade people that independence was the right choice.

The French Revolution

A violent upheaval in France beginning in 1789 destroyed the old royal government and aristocracy, and created a republic. Although the monarchy was later restored, the French Revolution showed that governments in Europe now needed the agreement of the people.

The old regime

In the 1770s France was still the greatest country in Europe. The French king still lived in grand style, but the royal government was out of touch with its subjects and, worse, it was bankrupt. The expensive wars of the past hundred years were partly to blame, and so was the system of taxation, in which the rich paid nothing and the growing middle class, which produced most of the nation's wealth, paid most. In the 1780s, bad harvests brought higher food prices, but lower wages. There was famine in Paris. People were in an angry mood.

New ideas

Times had changed. The rush of new ideas which had produced the exciting progress in science made people question the whole system of government and society, including religion. Philosophers like Voltaire (left) and Rousseau believed that all questions could be answered by human reason. Frenchmen who had fought in the American Revolution came home with the idea that government should depend on the will of the people, not a king. All over France, and especially in Paris, the idea of change was in the air.

The National Assembly

In this crisis, the royal government called a meeting of the Estates General in 1789. This contained representatives of the Three Estates – nobles, clergy and the middle classes (the Third Estate), who had not met for 164 years! When they met, the Third Estate took over and declared themselves a National Assembly. Ignoring the royal government, the National Assembly completely reformed France. A new constitution ended the special rights of the nobles and clergy, and declared all men to be equal in the eyes of the law. Church lands were taken over for the nation. All censorship ended. When the king tried to stop the meetings of the Third Estate by locking them out of their chamber, the members refused to obey and met instead in the royal tennis court. There was great excitement in France. In the name of 'liberty, equality and brotherhood', a completely new society was created. France changed more in two years than it had in two centuries.

△ The *Corvée*, a duty that forced peasants to work on the roads for no pay, was one of the many causes for anger at the royal government.

▽ A doctor named Guillotine invented a new machine for executing people. It was gruesome, but it was very quick. Thousands died by the guillotine during the Terror.

△ On 14 July 1789 a crowd stormed the Bastille, a royal fortress in Paris, an act that marks the beginning of the French Revolution. July 14 is now a French national holiday.

'The Terror'

Excitement soon began to get out of hand. Mobs in the country burned the castles of the nobility. Aristocrats fled abroad. In 1793 a more extreme government, led by Robespierre, gained power and launched a reign of terror against 'enemies of the Revolution'. Over 2,000 people, including the king and queen, were executed by the guillotine, a machine for chopping off heads. No one was safe – not even Robespierre, as events turned out, because he was overthrown and executed in 1794.

The rest of Europe looked on in horror. Other governments were terrified that the revolution might spread. War broke out between France and Austria, joined by Prussia and later Britain. The government called up ordinary citizens to fight, the first 'people's army'. Inspired by revolutionary patriotism, they defeated the professional soldiers of France's enemies.

In Paris, different governments came and went. They were less savage than Robespierre's, but inefficient. Strong leadership was needed and, ten years after the outbreak of the Revolution, a young general, Napoleon Bonaparte, seized power. The Revolution was over, but Europe would never be the same.

Napoleon's Europe

Napoleon gained power in France after the last government of the French Revolution was overthrown. For 15 years he dominated Europe as no one person had done since the emperors of Ancient Rome. His conquests helped to spread the French Revolution's ideas about freedom and equal rights for everyone to other countries.

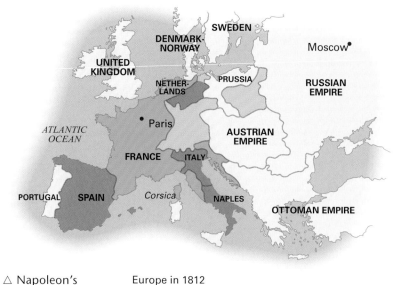

General and emperor

Napoleon Bonaparte was a brilliant young general in Revolutionary France when he came to power in 1799. France was then the enemy of all other states, whose rulers feared the republican ideas of the Revolution. In a series of campaigns, he defeated all the great continental powers – Austria, Prussia and Russia – and became master of Europe.

Napoleon was a skilful politician and diplomat. But as well as his own energy and ability Napoleon's real strength was the new citizen-army of France. He chose to fight his enemies in the open, avoiding the long and exhausting sieges of earlier wars. The French armies proved unbeatable on the battlefield. All the great powers were forced to make peace at one time or another, but the peace never lasted long because Napoleon's ambitions went on growing.

△ Napoleon's conquests brought huge changes to Europe. The Holy Roman Empire ceased to exist, after 1,000 years. Many small, independent German states disappeared. The French Empire became gigantic, and new 'puppet' states were created, some with Napoleon's relations on the throne.

Europe in 1812

- French Empire
- ruled by Napoleon's relations
- dependencies of France

▽ Napoleon at the battle of Austerlitz, 1805. For 14 years, he was never defeated on land.

▽ One of the practical reforms after the Revolution was the metric system. It was introduced in 1795. The original metre was a platinum bar, kept in Paris.

Napoleon's Europe

Crowned emperor in 1804, Napoleon had the powers of a dictator, and sometimes behaved like one. For example, he ended freedom of speech and sometimes imprisoned opponents without trial. But he also believed in the ideas of the Revolution, for example that men should be rewarded because of their achievements, rather than because of their noble birth. One improvement was his new, fairer law system, called the Napoleonic Code. This came to be used in South America and Japan as well as Europe.

Napoleon wanted to be not just a great military leader, but a great ruler of a peaceful empire. Under him, the whole system of government and education in France was reformed and brought under efficient, central control. In the long run these reforms were more important than his victories in battle. Napoleon's influence is still strong in France today.

△ Napoleon was a small man with enough fizz and energy for 100 men. His soldiers loved him, and the French people put up with constant war for the sake of glory.

France and Britain

Britain was Napoleon's most dangerous opponent. Napoleon was unbeatable on land, but Britain was protected by the sea. He tried to close all European ports to British trade, and the British navy replied by blockading French ports. He planned an invasion, and even collected barges in the Channel ports, but the British naval victory at Trafalgar (1805) made invasion impossible. While supporting Napoleon's enemies in Europe with money, Britain sent an army under the Duke of Wellington to help rebels against French rule in Spain and Portugal. There was a long, tough fight which held down some of Napoleon's forces. By 1813 Wellington had advanced into southern France.

Defeat

Napoleon's own ambition finally defeated him. In 1812 he invaded Russia, which was a huge and dangerous operation. He reached Moscow, but the Russians burned their own city, and the French pulled out. It was an extra-cold winter. Half a million Frenchmen died during the long retreat.

The disaster encouraged Napoleon's enemies to combine against him. He was defeated at Leipzig, his enemies invaded France, and he was sent into exile on a Mediterranean island (1814). A year later, he returned to Paris and regained control. He reigned 100 days, before his final defeat by Wellington at Waterloo.

The Pacific Lands

Australasia was the last continent to be settled by humans. It was also the last to be reached by European explorers. As in America, the Europeans soon took over.

△ We do not know exactly what the boats which the Polynesians used on their first Pacific voyages looked like, but they may have been like this modern version.

The first immigrants

The islands of the Pacific were settled by people from south-east Asia. The ancestors of the Aborigines arrived in Australia over 50,000 years ago, probably on rafts. The ancestors of the Polynesians, including the Maoris of New Zealand, came later, between 2,000 and 4,000 years ago. They travelled thousands of kilometres in sailing canoes. How they found the Pacific islands is a mystery.

European explorers

Portuguese and Dutch sailors landed on the coasts of Australia and New Zealand in the 17th century, usually by mistake. The British and French began to send expeditions to explore the region only in the 18th century. The greatest of these explorers was a British captain, James Cook. During his voyage of 1768-71 he sailed all around New Zealand and along eastern Australia, claiming it for Britain. Geographers believed there must be a giant southern continent in the south to balance the huge mass of Europe and Asia in the north. Cook proved that this did not exist.

△ Captain Cook (below) spent six months carefully mapping the coasts of New Zealand. Then he sailed along the east coast of Australia inside the Great Barrier Reef – a dangerous voyage for a sailing ship.

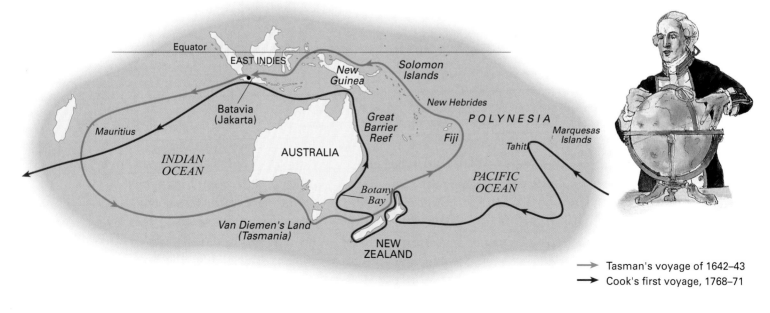

Tasman's voyage of 1642–43
Cook's first voyage, 1768–71

Australia

The Aborigines were a Stone Age people, who lived in large groups where everyone was related. They had no metals, and lived by hunting and gathering food. Men hunted using spears and boomerangs made of wood. They believed that human beings are part of nature, in the same way as trees, rocks and animals. Because they were often on the move, they had no proper houses and few clothes or belongings.

△ This fish was painted on rock by Aborigine artists at Obirr Rock. It almost looks like an X-ray of a fish.

New Zealand

The Maoris were more advanced in technology. They lived in fortified villages, growing crops, making clothes, and waging wars. Their main weapons were heavy wooden clubs, until the Europeans brought in guns, which made Maori wars far more deadly.

The Maoris loved dancing, feasts and ceremonies. They used feathers as decoration and, like other Polynesians, they practised tattooing. The skin was pricked, then vegetable dye was rubbed into the pricks, forming beautiful patterns.

△ Wooden forts protected Maori villages. Like all Polynesians, the Maoris were expert wood carvers and decorated their houses with complicated designs. Their clothes were woven by women in the village. Using a large swing was a popular pastime.

Convicts and colonists

The first British settlers in Australia were convicts, sent into exile at Botany Bay, and their guards. Other colonists followed, hoping for a new life. Though life was hard, they made a living catching whales. Raising sheep and cattle brought more profits, but this also took up the Aborigines' land and almost destroyed the old way of life. The Dutch explorer, Abel Janszoon Tasman, reached New Zealand in 1642 and was driven off by the Maoris. Later European sailors found a better welcome, but the first colonists did not arrive from Britain until after 1800.

The Industrial Revolution

Between 1800 and 1900 life in Western countries changed more, and more quickly, than ever before. The biggest change was from a world of villages and farms to one of cities and factories, where machines produced goods much faster than the old methods. This was a revolution as important as the French Revolution.

Life before the Industrial Revolution

In about 1750 most people still lived in the countryside. They produced most of their own food and made their own clothes. Goods were made in workshops by country craftsmen, as they had been for centuries. There were no factories, and the machines in use, such as looms for weaving cloth, had not changed much for centuries. They were still powered by human muscle. Goods were transported either by pack horses and wagons on country tracks, or by boats along rivers and on the growing number of canals.

Manpower and money

The Industrial Revolution was possible because by the mid-18th century there was enough money to set up factories and enough people to work in them. Capital – money for investment – was needed to build the factories, and banks could provide it thanks to the profits made in trade. In spite of wars, trade had been growing since the 16th century, especially in countries such as Britain and France. At the same time there were more men, women and children available to work in the new factories because the population was growing fast. More people needed more food, and this was provided by improvements in farming. Fewer people died young thanks to advances in health and medicine, which helped prevent diseases like plague.

Machines and factories

The first industry to be 'revolutionised' was the cotton industry in Britain. In the old system, cloth was made by spinners and weavers, who often worked in their own cottages. When the spinning jenny was invented, it made the task of spinning 100 times faster. That encouraged other people to invent machines to speed up the weaving process and the harvesting of raw cotton. In this way, one new invention led to others, and progress in one industry led to progress in others.

▷ Farming in the 18th century became more 'scientific'. New crops, new types of fertiliser, and new inventions such as the seed drill helped increase production. This huge sheep resulted from experiments in animal breeding.

The new machines were huge and needed a lot of power. They had to be kept in one building – a factory. The workers had to come to the factory, where they were supervised and everyone worked the same hours. In the factory, jobs became more specialised. Each worker performed one small job in the manufacturing process.

Power for the factories

Before the Industrial Revolution, simple machines were powered by watermills or windmills. The earliest factories were built beside rivers partly because they needed water power to drive their machines. But the power that made the Industrial Revolution work came from the steam engine. Steam engines of a sort had existed for many years. They were large, clumsy and inefficient, but useful for pumping water out of mines. In about 1770 a Scottish engineer, James Watt, produced a far better steam engine. Versions of Watt's engine powered the machines of the new factories.

△ One of the first steam machines was called 'the Miner's Friend', because it was used to pump water out of mines. Steam engines were too low powered and clumsy for most other jobs, until James Watt's improvements.

Fuel for the engines

Engines need fuel, and the fuel used by steam engines was coal. In coal mining, new machines were not so important. The main job was still done by men chopping away the coal face with pick axes. But now the number of coal miners increased from a few thousand to several million, as many new, deeper mines opened. Coal was also needed for the new type of blast furnaces in the iron industry, which became the most important heavy industry of the century.

◁ Until the 18th century, iron could only be made in small amounts. In the Industrial Revolution, it became the chief raw material of 'heavy' industry thanks to improvements in technology. James Nasmyth, a Scottish engineer like Watt, made many of them, including (left) his steam hammer (1839), for forging huge iron objects.

Advances in Transport

The Industrial Revolution depended on better and quicker ways of transporting raw materials and finished goods. Among the many ways that transport improved, the most important was the building of railways.

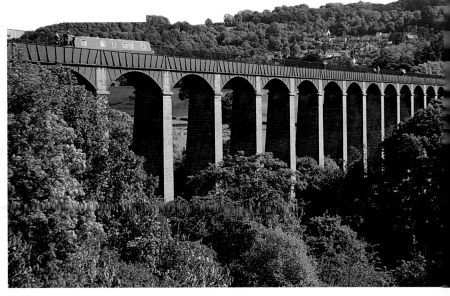

▽ The Pont Cysyllte Aqueduct (1805) in Wales. New engineering skills allowed canals to be carried across valleys on aqueducts and through mountains in tunnels.

Roads and canals

For thousands of years, the fastest way to travel was on a horse. Goods were carried by wagons or pack horses, but the roads were poor. Bigger loads, when possible, went by boat. New industries needed better transport. New roads and bridges were built and, more important, waterways were improved by making rivers fit for horse-drawn barges and by building canals.

Railways

Canals carried big loads at low cost, but they were slow. The answer to the transport problem in industrial countries was the railway. Wooden railways with trucks pulled by horses already existed in mines. Public railways linking towns and cities were made possible by the invention of reliable iron rails and by the locomotive – the mobile steam engine.

People in every country saw how important railways were for industrial development. The iron rails crossed Europe, North America and, soon, the rest of the world. At first, railways were often built by British companies. In 1870, about one mile in twenty of the world's railways, from Australia to Argentina, had been built by the British contractor Thomas Brassey. Other countries soon caught up. Railways were especially important in large countries such as the USA. Mines could be opened and factories started in places that had no water transport.

▽ More railways – about 200,000 miles of them – were built in the USA from 1865 to 1915 than anywhere else. When the Union Pacific line was completed in 1869, it became possible to travel from the Atlantic to the Pacific coast by train.

Ships

Transport by sea was already much more efficient than transport by land, and many years passed before iron steamships took over from sail. For a long voyage with a large cargo, sailing ships were best. Paddle steamers were seen on rivers in the 1820s. But at sea, steamers were a rare sight until after 1840, when the screw propeller was invented. Even then they still had sails as well as an engine. In steamships, cargo space had to be used to store coal for the engines, and on very long voyages steam ships had to stop to refuel.

The Suez Canal between the Mediterranean and the Red Sea opened in 1869. It reduced the sailing distance from Europe to the Far East by 8,000 km, which gave steamships a big advantage.

△ The USS *Savannah* crossed the Atlantic in 1819, using her steam engine for a few hours only. The real breakthrough was the *Great Britain*, the first large iron ship, the largest ship in the world, with a screw propeller. She crossed in 1845.

Communications

New inventions, made possible by scientific discoveries, also speeded up communication between people. The first good telegraph system, a method of sending messages electrically by wire, was started by an American, Samuel F. B. Morse. It used the dot-dash code that he invented. The telephone (above), invented about 1875, was even better than the telegraph, allowing people in different cities to talk directly to each other.

Industrial Society

The Industrial Revolution made some people rich. It also created a new kind of society, with huge new problems. Because it had happened fast, there were no laws or organisations to deal with these problems.

Factories and slums

To a traveller in Europe about 1850, country districts showed little sign of change. But in the industrial cities, everything was new and strange. Thousands of people worked in factories that were noisy, dirty and dangerous. Work was boring, hours were long – 12 hours a day or more – and wages were low. The coal mines were even worse. Miners often worked by candlelight, which could cause explosions. They had no helmets, and they were lowered down the mineshaft, perhaps 300m deep, on ropes.

The industrial workers lived in crowded houses. Sometimes a whole family had to share one room. The houses were built as quickly and cheaply as possible, without proper drains, running water or even fresh air. For the poor there were no parks, no schools, no entertainment, no holidays with pay, no sickness benefit, no unemployment pay. Of course, craftsmen and farm workers had none of these things either. What was new and shocking in industrial slums was the size of the problem.

△ Factory smoke over a steel-making town in Pennsylvania, USA, in about 1900. Industrial cities grew from country towns or villages in a few years. The noise, smoke, dirt and slums struck outsiders with horror.

◁ Children did not have to go to school. Poor children went to work at an early age, sometimes five or six. Dangerous machines, like this mechanical loom, were unguarded and accidents were common.

Rich and poor

In the end, industrialisation made almost everyone better off. But at first it made a few people rich, while others were so poor they did not have enough to eat. The purpose of industrial society was to make profits. Employers believed that to make their profits as large as possible, workers' wages should be as low as possible. A few wise people saw that this was not even true, such as the reformer Robert Owen. He set up a factory in Scotland with decent conditions and good homes. Unfortunately, few bosses copied him. A capitalist with money to invest looked around for some profitable business. He seldom invested in projects such as better housing, which were really needed, because they would not make him a big profit.

Working people had no power and in most European countries were forbidden to form trade unions to try to improve wages and conditions. But some people remembered the power of the city crowd during the French Revolution. In Lyons, weavers and other workers rebelled in 1831, in 1834 and again in 1849.

▷ Machine breaking. The new machines made many skilled workers unemployed. In some parts, gangs of angry people attacked the machines, and sometimes the factory bosses too.

Emigration

In the 19th century the population grew faster than ever. In 1800 Europe had about 180 million people, but by 1900 there were about 400 million, mostly living in cities. The real increase was even larger, but many Europeans emigrated, like these Italian families on the first stage of their journey to Canada. Besides North America, they went to Australia and other countries, whose populations grew even faster. Millions of people fled Ireland to escape starvation in 1845-46 when the potato crop failed.

Government action

The problems of industrial society were so great, they could only be solved by new laws. Governments were slow to act, but after about 1820 they passed laws to improve housing and working conditions. Factory inspectors enforced the rules. Working time was reduced, child labour stopped, and trade unions were allowed. Local governments collected rubbish, built sewers and supplied clean water. Cleaner cities brought better health. Outbreaks of cholera, which had killed thousands, ended. In Prussia, laws were passed in the 1880s to help the old and sick. By 1900, living standards were rising.

Reform and Revolt

The ideas of the French Revolution and the growth of a new middle class in industrialised countries led to demands for more democratic government. In most countries, the struggle for power was violent.

Europe after Napoleon

In 1815, the leaders of Europe met at the Congress of Vienna to sort out Europe's affairs after the defeat of Napoleon. As far as possible, they tried to restore the old Europe, where governments were controlled by kings and nobles. This could not last. Two great forces opposed the old system. The first was nationalism, the idea that states should be independent nations, not part of a foreign empire. Most people who believed in nationalism also believed in liberalism, the second great force for change in 19th-century Europe.

1848 – the year of revolutions

Between 1815 and 1848 many revolts broke out against royal governments. The biggest outbreak came in 1848, with uprisings in nearly every European country. France became a republic again, and other governments were forced to give more power to the people. But the French Second Republic lasted only four years before its president, who was a nephew of Napoleon, made himself emperor as Napoleon III (above). None of the revolutions of 1848 succeeded in bringing about equality or democratic government, but they did reduce the powers of the old, anti-liberal governments over their citizens. Although Europe had no more 'years of revolution' after 1848, liberal reforms came slowly. In 1900 there were still only two republics in Europe – Switzerland and the French Third Republic (founded after Napoleon III's defeat in 1870).

▽ Some protests in 1848 were peaceful. There was no violence in Britain, for example. Here, German workers present a petition demanding liberal reforms to the local government. In German states, one common demand was for a united country.

Liberalism

Liberalism means freedom. In politics, it meant more freedom for ordinary people to take part in government. With that went other freedoms, such as freedom to say what you believed without fear of arrest, or to follow any religion you chose. Liberalism was strong among the new middle class and skilled tradesmen. Liberals also wanted less government control. This idea made it difficult for governments to deal with the problems caused by the Industrial Revolution, especially the poor living conditions of industrial workers.

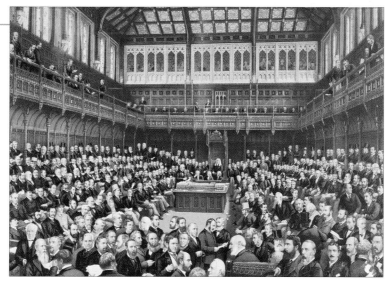

△ The British House of Commons in 1888. Parliament had been the most powerful part of government since the 17th century, but it was still controlled by rich landowners until the Reform Acts.

Peaceful reform

Liberal reformers looked to Great Britain as an example. Britain had a long tradition of parliamentary government. Power was held not by the monarch, but by parliament. Britain was the most liberal of the larger powers. However, before 1832 very few Britons had the right to vote in elections to parliament. A huge city like Manchester had no members of parliament, while some small villages had two. The Reform Act (1832) made voting more fair, and later reform acts (1867 and 1884) gave more men the vote.

Socialism

Socialism was a growing force in 19th-century Europe. Socialists wanted to give power to working people by taking away the wealth and property of the small number of people at the top. In a socialist state, everyone would be equal. All property would be owned by the state on behalf of the people. All profits from business would go to the state, for the good of the people. Some socialists, including Karl Marx, believed that this kind of state could be won only by a violent revolution of the working class against the middle and upper classes. Marx's *Communist Manifesto* was published in 1848, but had little effect until later. Other socialists believed in peaceful reform, by legal, democratic means. Socialists opposed liberalism just as strongly as they opposed royal governments.

Education

The new, industrial working class was weak not just because they could not vote, but because they were uneducated (most socialist leaders, like Marx, were middle-class by birth). By 1900, this was changing. Many European governments had come to realise that everyone should be educated. No longer was education left to the Church. Each country had a national system of education. Primary education (up to age 12 or 14) was usually free, and every girl and boy had to go to school. Secondary and higher education also expanded, because industrial countries needed more skilled people. Many new universities and technical colleges were founded. But these advances were slower in eastern Europe. More than half the people of Russia in 1917 could not read or write.

△ With education for all, everyone could read the news for themselves and form their own opinions.

Australia and New Zealand

In the 19th century, nearly all the islands in the Pacific were under European rule. The largest land masses, Australia and New Zealand, attracted many European settlers. As in North America, these settlers founded new nations.

Australia

New South Wales began to do well and attract colonists when sheep pastures were found to the west of Sydney. More colonies were started privately around the coasts of Australia. For the sake of law and order, the British government soon took them over. But they remained separate colonies, with their own governments, and even different widths of railway line. These colonies became states and joined together as a nation only in 1901.

Australia is bigger than the whole of Europe, not counting Russia, and for many years the colonists did not travel far from the coast. When they began to explore the centre, they found mostly hot, harsh desert. The explorers Burke and Wills were the first to travel across Australia, from south to north (1861). Only one member of their expedition got home alive. No one tried to start new settlements in central Australia. But things changed when gold was discovered in the 1850s. Mining towns sprang up, thousands of prospectors arrived from North America, China and Britain, hoping to get rich, The population began to grow at a much faster rate.

▷ This Australian poster of 1816, in picture language, promised that whites would be hanged for killing 'blacks' as well as blacks for killing whites. But white settlers often committed violence without being punished. Some hunted the Aborigines like animals, and almost destroyed the ancient way of life before they even understood it.

New Zealand

The first European settlements in New Zealand were camps made by the crews of whaling ships and traders from Australia. British missionaries and colonists followed. Reports of cruelty against the native people, the Maori, resulted in the British government taking over. This encouraged more British settlers to come, but did not prevent wars over land. In the Treaty of Waitangi (1840), Maori leaders agreed to accept British rule in return for a promise that their rights would be protected. This promise was not kept. The discovery of gold later in the century and the good farming land attracted still more settlers, mostly from Britain.

◁ In spite of the British government's promises, settlers in New Zealand's North Island took over lands that belonged to Maori tribes. The result was a series of wars in 1860-72, in which the Maori were eventually defeated. They lost their independence and much of their land.

▽ European colonies in south-east Asia and the Pacific at the end of the 19th century.

Exports

Australia and New Zealand traded farming products, such as wool and meat. Their main market was Britain, which also supplied the goods they needed to import. Britain was far away, and only goods that would not perish could be exported. In 1880 a new technology changed that: refrigeration. As frozen meat could be exported, sheep farmers could export mutton as well as wool; also beef, butter and cheese. By 1890 Australia had one sixth of the world's sheep.

New nations

Both Australia and New Zealand remained closely tied to Britain. Their national income came chiefly from trade with Britain, and they had few links with nearer neighbours such as China and Japan. Although both gained their own, independent governments, they remained loyal members of the British Empire. Most newer immigrants were British, and the Australian government refused to admit non-Europeans until 1945.

Europeans in the Pacific

Besides the British, the French were also active in the Pacific. They claimed many groups of small islands, and took over Vietnam and Cambodia on the Asian mainland. Most of modern Indonesia was officially Dutch, although the Dutch never explored it all. The 7,000 islands of the Philippines, part of the Spanish empire since the 16th century, were taken over by the USA in 1898.

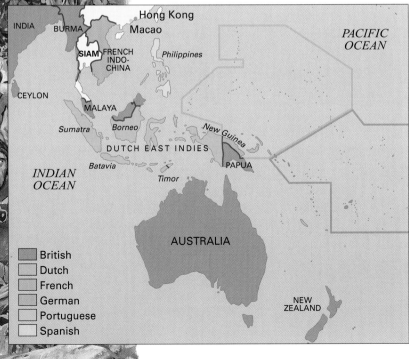

INDIA
BURMA
Hong Kong
Macao
SIAM
FRENCH INDO-CHINA
Philippines
PACIFIC OCEAN
CEYLON
MALAYA
Sumatra
Borneo
New Guinea
DUTCH EAST INDIES
Batavia
Timor
PAPUA
INDIAN OCEAN
AUSTRALIA
NEW ZEALAND

British
Dutch
French
German
Portuguese
Spanish

The American Civil War

The American Civil War began when the Southern states tried to leave the Union, which the federal government refused to accept. The defeat of the South, after four years of fighting and one million deaths, resulted in the end of slavery and a stronger union under Northern control.

North vs. South

The union of American states had been created to fight the British, and was never strong. The sharpest division was between the farming South, which depended on cotton produced by slaves, and the industrial North, where slavery was illegal. Some Northerners believed slavery should be abolished in the South too. The different views on slavery caused serious conflict as the country expanded westward. In the new territory of Kansas, fighting broke out between supporters and opponents of slavery. In politics, tempers were high. The Democratic Party, which depended on support in North and South, split in two, for and against slavery, each with its own candidate for president. As a result, the 1860 election was won by Abraham Lincoln, candidate of the Republicans, a new party of Northerners which was strongly against slavery in the South.

Many Southerners believed that the Republicans would end slavery, taking away their workforce, and feared the blacks would attack them. Before Lincoln had entered the White House, the Southern states officially withdrew from the Union and founded the Confederate States of America. When the Confederates attacked a federal fort at Fort Sumter, South Carolina, in April 1861, the Civil War began.

■ Confederate States
■ Union States
□ territories not yet states

△ The Northern (Union) and Southern (Confederate) states. The war was important for other countries too. For example, most of the cotton used in European factories came from the South. When the war stopped cotton imports, thousands of workers lost their jobs.

War

The Union had big advantages over the Confederates: more men, more money, most of the industry and railways. They also had control of the navy, which prevented the Confederates getting help from abroad. But the Confederates had great fighting spirit and, at first, better generals. Besides, they only had to defend the South, while the Union had to invade and conquer it. As a result, the war lasted four years, before the Confederates were forced to surrender.

◁ Although the Confederacy had no navy, it had two or three warships. Most famous was the *Alabama*, a sailing ship with a steam engine. Her career lasted two years, and she captured or destroyed about 70 Union merchant ships. In June 1864 she fought her final duel with a Union frigate in the English Channel, and was sunk.

◁ At the Battle of Chattanooga in November 1863, Union forces led by General Grant defeated the Confederates in a decisive confrontation. The Union could now use Chattanooga, in Tennesee, as a base for General Sherman's invasion of Georgia.

Events of the Civil War

1861 February: Jefferson Davis is elected president of the Confederacy.
April: Confederates attack Fort Sumter.
July: Confederate victory at Bull Run.

1862 August: Confederates under General Lee invade the North.
October: Lee's advance is checked.

1863 January: Lincoln proclaims the freedom of slaves.
July: Union victory at Gettysburg.
November: Lincoln delivers his Gettysburg Address in praise of unity and democracy.

1864 Union army under Sherman invades Georgia and burns Atlanta.

1865 Confederate commander Robert E. Lee surrenders to General Ulysses S. Grant at Appomatox.

The end of slavery

Some slaves escaped to the North, some were Union spies, and some joined the army. In 1862 President Lincoln's Emancipation Proclamation declared an end to slavery, causing celebrations among the slaves (below). About 4 million slaves became legally free, but they had no money and no property, and still depended on their former owners. Even in many northern states, blacks were not allowed to vote in elections until after 1870. A long struggle for equality lay ahead.

Asians and Europeans

During the 19th century the influence of Europe and the USA spread throughout the world. Some countries, such as China, tried to resist this, while others, such as Japan, adopted Western methods and ideas.

▽ For centuries, Europeans were amazed by the civilisation of China. But in the 19th century, China seemed backward. It still had beautiful arts and crafts, but it was helpless before the power and energy of the industrial West.

Rebellion in China

The Chinese Empire was bigger than Europe, but the Qing government was weak and losing control. During the Taiping Rebellion, from 1850 to 1864, rebels controlled most of central China. The country was in chaos. In the north, millions died of famine. But the imperial court blocked all efforts by Chinese officials to reform the government.

China and the West

The rebels gained extra support from the government's feeble dealings with the West. Once, China had been ahead of Europe in many ways. Now, it was far behind. But the Chinese still believed that other nations were 'barbarians'. For thousands of years the Chinese had considered their civilisation superior. Immigrants, like the Qing themselves, soon became 'Chinese'.

But the Europeans were different. They bought tea from China and, in exchange, tried to force the Chinese to buy goods from them. One thing the Chinese people were ready to buy was opium, a drug forbidden by their government. British efforts to sell opium, which was grown in Bengal, led to two 'opium wars' (1839-42 and 1856-60). China was easily defeated. Beijing was looted by French and British troops, and China was forced to open its ports to Western trade. Many cities came under Western control. Hong Kong became a British colony, Russia seized land in the north, and France took over Indo-China (Vietnam, Laos and Cambodia).

The Boxer Rebellion

The 'Righteous Fists' or Boxers, as Westerners called them, were a secret society united by hatred of Western influence. Their rebellion in 1900 was not against the Chinese government, but against the foreigners who seemed to be taking over China. The Boxers killed Christian Chinese, as well as Western missionaries, and attacked the embassies of Western governments in Beijing. Their rebellion was crushed by European, not Chinese, forces.

The Republic

It looked as though the whole of China would be carved up among the Western powers. But in 1911, the Chinese reformers won at last. The last emperor was deposed, and a republic was created under Sun Zhong Shan (Sun Yat-sen), leader of the Guomindang or Nationalist party.

Japan's emperor restored

After the USA had forced Japan to open trade with the West in 1858, the ruling Tokugawa were overthrown and the Meiji emperor was restored to power. The new Japanese leaders were determined to make Japan rich and powerful, and the way they did it was by learning the lessons of the West. Government, laws, and schools were completely changed as Japan followed Western examples.

▽ The Russo-Japanese War showed that an Asian country could be a great power. At the battle of Tsushima (1905), a huge Russian fleet was destroyed by Japan's up-to-date warships.

▽ Some Japanese welcomed Western ideas. This lady has a western husband and western clothes.

Japan and the West

The Japanese government did all it could to encourage industry and trade. It built a national railway network to improve travel between the mountainous Japanese islands. The special rights of the old warrior class, the samurai, were ended. Instead, a modern people's army was created.

By 1900 Japan was the equal of the West as an industrial country. But Japanese leaders also intended to make their country an imperial power. In 1894-95 Japan fought a successful war against China, gaining Taiwan. In another war in 1904-5, Japan fought Russia in Korea and in China's northern province of Manchuria. It seemed impossible that a small Asian country could beat a huge European power, but Japan won every important battle.

Nationalism

A powerful force in the 19th century was the idea that nations – groups of people who spoke the same language – should rule their own country. Some of the old empires, made up of many nations, were breaking up. New nation-states grew from the pieces.

▷ Garibaldi captured the Kingdom of the Two Sicilies with about 1,000 of his famous 'Redshirts'. (He had led them in a war in Uruguay, and they brought their red shirts to Europe with them.) They were helped by many local risings.

New European nations

One of the first new nations in Europe was Belgium. This independent kingdom was formed when the Belgians rebelled against their ruler, the king of Holland, in 1830. The Catholic Belgians were divided from the Protestant Dutch by religion, as well as by language differences.

Religion was also the main cause of the Greeks' fight against the Ottoman Turks. Greece won independence in 1830, and was the first of the Balkan countries to break away from Turkish rule. The Ottoman Empire was now weak. It continued to exist only because rival European powers supported it, to stop each other taking over the Turks' European provinces. This rivalry caused the Crimean War (1852-54), when Britain and France fought against Russia. But although new nations were being created, not all nationalist revolts were successful.

△ The Greeks kept their national customs and culture, even under Turkish rule.

Italy

After 1848, the *Risorgimento*, or 'rebirth', of Italy was led by the kingdom of Sardinia, in north-west Italy. It was directed by a skilful statesman, Count Cavour, and supported by France. Meanwhile, in the south, a rebellion began against the conservative rulers of the Kingdom of the Two Sicilies. The leader of this revolt was a patriotic adventurer, Giuseppe Garibaldi. He had also fought for freedom in South America and was an inspiring figure. The northern and southern movements combined to create a united Italy in 1862. The king of Sardinia became king of Italy. But Rome was still ruled by the Pope. He refused to give up the city, but he had no army to defend it. In 1870 the new government took Rome, which became the capital.

Dates of Independence in Latin America

1811 Colombia	1821 Mexico
Ecuador	Peru
Venezeula	1822 Brazil
Paraguay	1823 Central
1814 Uruguay	America
1816 Argentina	1825 Bolivia
1818 Chile	

Latin America

Beginning with Haiti in 1804, most Latin American countries gained independence before 1830. In South America, the rebels against Spanish rule were usually Creoles, middle-class people of European descent. Their greatest leader was Símon Bolívar (left), who created 'Gran Colombia'. It was later split into separate states, ending the dream of making the old Spanish province of New Granada into one large nation. However, after Brazil gained independence from Portugal, it remained one country, a state larger than the USA. In Mexico, peasants and poor people took part in the fight for independence, as well as Creoles.

A united Germany

The main German-speaking states were Protestant Prussia, in the north, and Catholic Austria (the old Habsburg empire) in the south. Which one would unite the German nation? Guided by the great statesman, Bismarck, Prussia proved the stronger. Bismarck brought about a war with Austria, and Prussia won in four weeks. Prussia's influence now increased in the Catholic south, as well as the Protestant north. The Austrian Empire, with its many non-German peoples, was weakened by nationalist revolts, especially in Italy and Hungary. The Hungarians gained their own government in 1867.

The power of Prussia alarmed the French. In 1870, again through Bismarck's schemes, war broke out with France. In six weeks, France was defeated and in despair at the loss of its northern provinces, Alsace and Lorraine. On a tide of German nationalist excitement, a German empire was declared. The king of Prussia became emperor of Germany, with the trusty Bismarck as his chancellor. A great new national state had been created, larger and stronger than France or even Britain.

▽ Steel works at Essen, Germany, 1910. The division of Germany delayed trade and industrial development. After 1871 it caught up fast. By 1900 it had passed Britain as the leading industrial state in Europe.

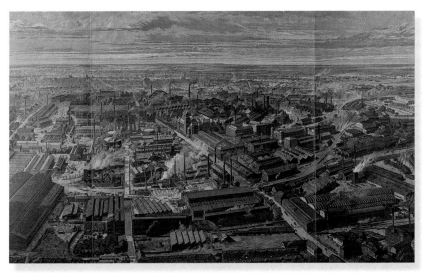

The Scramble for Africa

While small nations in Europe were fighting against the empires that ruled them, Europeans were taking over on other continents. By 1914, 80 percent of the world was ruled by 'Westerners' – Europeans or their descendants.

Europeans in Africa

In 1880 Europeans controlled little of Africa, except South Africa. In the next 20 years almost the whole continent came under European rule. The 'scramble' for colonies began when King Leopold of the Belgians gained the Congo, as a huge estate for himself. Then Germany, a new nation with no colonies, grabbed territories in four different parts. In the north, the weakness of the Ottoman Empire allowed France to move into North Africa and Britain into Egypt. A European conference in Berlin (1885) recognised Leopold's right to the Congo and encouraged rivals, especially Britain and France, to divide up the continent.

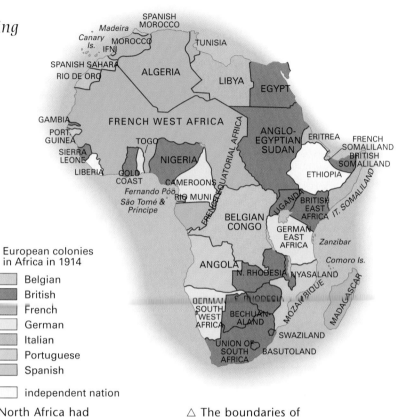

European colonies in Africa in 1914

- Belgian
- British
- French
- German
- Italian
- Portuguese
- Spanish
- independent nation

▽ North Africa had been part of Arab-Islamic civilisation for centuries. After the French conquest, many French people settled in Algeria. This would cause trouble in the future.

△ The boundaries of colonies were drawn by statesmen in Europe, who knew almost nothing about the peoples living in the regions they were dividing up.

Colonies in Africa

Most European governments did not really want new colonies in unknown lands. So why did they take them? Businessmen hoped for new opportunities. Missionaries longed to spread Christianity. Governments were afraid of a rival power gaining a position from which it could threaten their trade. Also, a nation that saw its neighbours winning foreign empires felt that they should do the same. Few colonists considered the wishes of the people they came to rule. Many believed that by bringing them Western civilisation, including Christianity, they were doing the Africans a favour.

South Africa

The British took over the Dutch colony at the Cape of Good Hope in 1814, to protect the sea route to India. British settlers began to arrive. The Afrikaners, descendants of the early Dutch settlers, disliked British control. Beginning in 1836, many left the Cape to get away from it. They set up home in Natal, in spite of clashes with the Zulu, a warlike people who later defeated British professional soldiers in a few battles. When the British took over Natal, the Afrikaners moved on again. In Transvaal they still could not escape the British and other foreigners, who flooded in when gold and diamonds were discovered there.

The South African War

Disagreements between the British and Afrikaners finally led to the South African War of 1899. For a few thousand farmers to take on the mighty British Empire seemed crazy, but the Afrikaners held out for three years before finally giving up the unequal fight. The peace treaty (1902) recognised British rule, and led to a union of all the South African territories, including Cape Colony, in 1910. The Union of South Africa then joined Canada, Australia and New Zealand as Dominions governing themselves in the British Empire.

▽ Beginning in 1836, thousands of Afrikaner families, travelling in ox wagons, took part in the Great Trek from the Cape to the north-west. They crossed the Drakensberg Mountains in search of fresh grazing land and freedom from the British.

Ashanti

Ashanti was a small but powerful kingdom in West Africa. Its symbol was a Golden Stool (below). Quarrels with the British over trade led to war. Ashanti won the first war, in 1824, but when it again attacked British trading posts it was defeated. In 1901 the British took over the Ashanti kingdom, to strengthen their position in West Africa against the French.

The Growth of the USA

In the second half of the 19th century all Western countries grew richer and stronger at an amazing rate. The country that grew fastest was the USA. By 1900 it was the richest country in the world.

The American West

The West filled up with settlers, and the population increased rapidly. The Homestead Act (1862) gave pioneer families 160 acres of land free if they lived on it for five years.

Cities grew even faster. Cities like Cincinnati grew up on the profits of the meat industry. Herds of cattle now grazed on the plains where once the bison had roamed. A new kind of wheat was developed for the prairie soil, and farmers produced so much grain that world prices fell sharply.

▷ The Statue of Liberty, 46 metres high, was erected in New York harbour in 1885. It was designed by a French sculptor and was a gift from the French to the people of the USA. This great landmark became the first sight of New York for poor immigrants from Europe.

The Indian wars

As millions of farmers and mining prospectors swarmed across the American West, the Native Americans were either killed or crowded into reservations. Wars against the Sioux, Cheyenne and other peoples, which lasted from 1864 to 1886, finally destroyed their way of life. One of the greatest leaders in the Indian wars was Sitting Bull (left), a chief of the Sioux. He took part in the battle of Little Bighorn (1876), where US cavalry, commanded by General Custer, were defeated.

California

In the 1840s California belonged to Mexico, although a few hundred US citizens lived there. In 1848, after the US-Mexican war, California passed to the USA. In the same year, a settler in California discovered gold. The population doubled in a few months, as thousands of people hurried to join in the gold rush. The gold did not last long, but by the 1860s California was doing well from farming, especially fruit, which (after 1869) could be carried across the continent by rail.

The railway

The 'Iron Horse', as people called the railway engine, seemed an amazing machine. Some people believed it would help to unite America, after the Civil War, by joining north and south, east and west. By 1860, the USA had nearly half of all the railways in the world, and lines had reached the growing towns of the Middle West. A link to the Pacific Ocean was completed in 1869. About 20,000 men worked on it, laying 1,775 miles of track in three years.

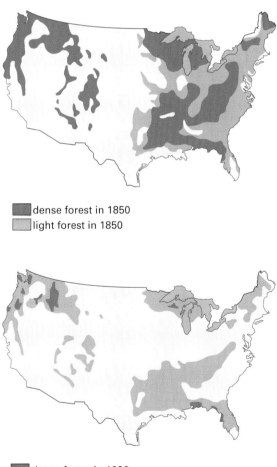

■ dense forest in 1850
▨ light forest in 1850

■ dense forest in 1926
▨ light forest in 1926

△ When the first colonists arrived, half the country was covered with forest. Today, only small patches are left.

Industry

After the Civil War the US government encouraged business and industry, and ambitious men travelled the continent looking for ways to make money. In spite of its problems, the country was in a hopeful mood. Factories and mines developed, helped by the railways which opened up new regions. Vast new industries, such as steel and oil, rose in town and country. These industries provided many jobs, although most people working in them were poorly paid. The big trade unions were formed in the 1880s to campaign for the rights of industrial workers, and wages started to rise.

△ Andrew Carnegie (1835-1919) was born into a poor Scottish family, that emigrated to the USA when he was 13. He built a huge steel business, and was so rich he was able to give $350 million to charity.

The people who owned the new industries became millionaires. Their wealth gave them great influence. Some tycoons misused this power and bribed judges and politicians for favours. The big corporations controlled the market and set prices. Small businesses could not compete with them, and were soon taken over or forced to close. It was not until the 1900s that the US government took action, passing laws to control business and make sure prices were fair.

The Poor

Although clever and ruthless men could make a fortune quickly, many other people were not well off. The blacks may have been free, but they were denied many basic rights. The Native Americans were crowded into special 'reservations' on the poorest land. They were controlled by the US government, which had to supply them with food, because they could no longer hunt. Many poor European immigrants, such as Irish and Italians, who entered the country in millions, struggled to live in city slums.

Science

Human beings came to understand far more about the Earth, nature and themselves in the 19th century. Scientific discoveries led to new industries and, for many people, a longer and healthier life.

Life on Earth

Most Christians in 1800 believed God had created the Earth a few thousand years earlier and little had changed since. Already, some people thought differently. The growth of sciences like biology and geology showed that the Earth was very old and had changed many times. The seas and continents had changed shape and, as fossils proved, different kinds of animals and plants existed in past ages. These discoveries gave rise to the theory of evolution, that all living things change, over millions of years.

▷ Advances in engineering and new materials produced new kinds of buildings. Brooklyn Bridge in New York was an early suspension bridge (opened in 1883). Its deck, 486 metres long, is suspended between towers. The skyscrapers were built later.

Scientists and inventors

This was an exciting and hopeful time. It seemed that all human problems would one day be solved by education and science. Even crime and poverty might disappear, thanks to greater knowledge and better education. In 1800 many modern sciences hardly existed. Schools and universities had few science classes. Many scientific discoveries were made by men and women who were not professional scientists. Inventions were made by craftsmen, not by experts in white coats. The first pedal bicycle was made by a Scottish blacksmith in his forge. Daguerre, the pioneer of photography, was a painter of scenery.

Technology

By 1900 enormous changes had taken place in industrial societies. Transport had gone from the horse and carriage to the train and the motor car. The first aeroplanes were a few years away. New kinds of buildings had appeared, made from new materials. The French engineer Gustave Eiffel built iron bridges across deep valleys before astonishing the world with his famous Tower in Paris (1889). Lighting had changed from candles to electric lamps.

1791 While dissecting a frog's leg, Luigi Galvani notices that an electric spark makes it twitch. This leads to the discovery of electric current.

1800 Alessandro Volta makes the first electric cell battery.

1823 Mathematician Charles Babbage designs what he calls an 'analytical engine', forerunner of the computer.

1826 Joseph Niépce and Louis Daguerre get together to make an early type of photograph.

1831-36 Charles Darwin (right) studies animals in South America, and develops his ideas of how evolution works by natural selection.

1831 Michael Faraday explains how a magnet can produce electricity, leading to the electrical generator.

1842 US surgeon Crawford Long uses ether as an anaesthetic, to put his patient to sleep.

1844 Samuel F. B. Morse sends the first message by telegraph on

a wire between Washington and Baltimore, USA.

1856 Henry Bessemer's converter allows steel to be made cheaply and in large amounts.

1859 Darwin finally publishes his book about evolution, *On the Origin of Species*.

Medicine

By 1900 people lived longer, and fewer people died while they were still young. The greatest advance in medicine was made by a French chemist, Louis Pasteur, who was trying to find out why wine sometimes went bad. He discovered that tiny organisms were to blame. Later, he proved that such organisms – germs – cause disease. It then became possible to inoculate people against many infectious diseases.

About 1865 a British surgeon, Joseph Lister, read about Pasteur's theory of germs. He guessed that germs might also cause infection in surgery, and developed the first antiseptics. Having an operation became less dangerous. It also became less painful, now that anaesthetics were in use.

▷ One of the first operations using an anaesthetic, ether, to put the patient to sleep. (This is a reconstruction, posed by actors.)

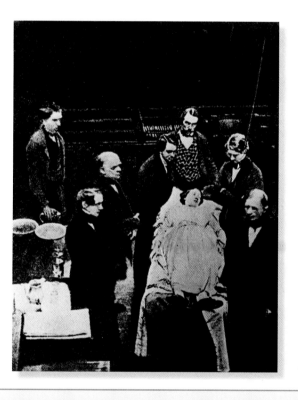

Health and hygiene

Hospitals also improved because of better nursing. Florence Nightingale set up the first modern school of nursing in 1860, and insisted that sick people needed clean beds and good food as well as well-trained nurses. The work of Pasteur and others showed that the greatest cause of disease and bad health is dirt, where germs breed. The industrial cities had no clean water, no sewers, and no street cleaning. Infectious diseases spread quickly. One outbreak of cholera in Britain in 1848 killed 130,000 people. The cities had to be cleaned up. Gradually, water supplies improved and new drains and sewers were built. One result was that cholera disappeared.

1860 French chemist Louis Pasteur shows that diseases are caused by bacteria.

1876 Alexander Graham Bell invents the telephone in the US and makes the first call, to his assistant in another room: "Mr. Watson, come here, I want you."

1876 US inventor Thomas Edison (below) makes a phonograph, forerunner of the record player.

1885 German engineer Karl Benz makes one of the first petrol (gasoline)-driven motor cars (right).

1895 Guglielmo Marconi sends the first 'wireless' message across a garden - the beginning of radio. In 1901 he sends a signal across the Atlantic.

1895 The Lumière brothers in France show one of the first forms of motion picture (right).

1895 German physicist Wilhelm von Röntgen discovers X-rays.

The Modern World

The modern world began with two kinds of revolution. Political revolutions in North America and France were based on the idea that governments should rule with the agreement of their people. In America, the result was a republic. France returned to royal

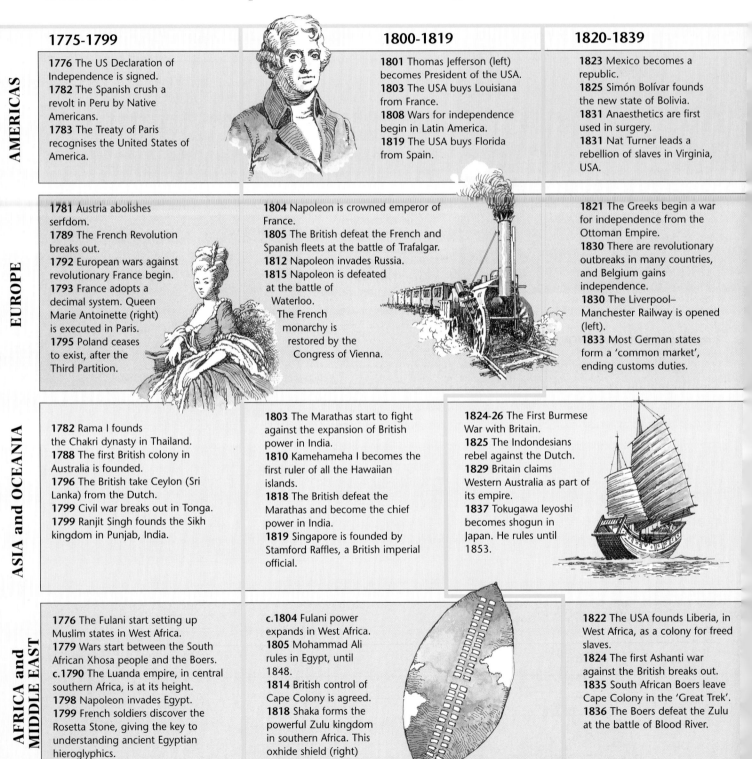

1775-1799

AMERICAS

1776 The US Declaration of Independence is signed.
1782 The Spanish crush a revolt in Peru by Native Americans.
1783 The Treaty of Paris recognises the United States of America.

EUROPE

1781 Austria abolishes serfdom.
1789 The French Revolution breaks out.
1792 European wars against revolutionary France begin.
1793 France adopts a decimal system. Queen Marie Antoinette (right) is executed in Paris.
1795 Poland ceases to exist, after the Third Partition.

ASIA and OCEANIA

1782 Rama I founds the Chakri dynasty in Thailand.
1788 The first British colony in Australia is founded.
1796 The British take Ceylon (Sri Lanka) from the Dutch.
1799 Civil war breaks out in Tonga.
1799 Ranjit Singh founds the Sikh kingdom in Punjab, India.

AFRICA and MIDDLE EAST

1776 The Fulani start setting up Muslim states in West Africa.
1779 Wars start between the South African Xhosa people and the Boers.
c.1790 The Luanda empire, in central southern Africa, is at its height.
1798 Napoleon invades Egypt.
1799 French soldiers discover the Rosetta Stone, giving the key to understanding ancient Egyptian hieroglyphics.

1800-1819

1801 Thomas Jefferson (left) becomes President of the USA.
1803 The USA buys Louisiana from France.
1808 Wars for independence begin in Latin America.
1819 The USA buys Florida from Spain.

1804 Napoleon is crowned emperor of France.
1805 The British defeat the French and Spanish fleets at the battle of Trafalgar.
1812 Napoleon invades Russia.
1815 Napoleon is defeated at the battle of Waterloo. The French monarchy is restored by the Congress of Vienna.

1803 The Marathas start to fight against the expansion of British power in India.
1810 Kamehameha I becomes the first ruler of all the Hawaiian islands.
1818 The British defeat the Marathas and become the chief power in India.
1819 Singapore is founded by Stamford Raffles, a British imperial official.

c.1804 Fulani power expands in West Africa.
1805 Mohammad Ali rules in Egypt, until 1848.
1814 British control of Cape Colony is agreed.
1818 Shaka forms the powerful Zulu kingdom in southern Africa. This oxhide shield (right) was made by the Zulu.

1820-1839

1823 Mexico becomes a republic.
1825 Simón Bolívar founds the new state of Bolivia.
1831 Anaesthetics are first used in surgery.
1831 Nat Turner leads a rebellion of slaves in Virginia, USA.

1821 The Greeks begin a war for independence from the Ottoman Empire.
1830 There are revolutionary outbreaks in many countries, and Belgium gains independence.
1830 The Liverpool–Manchester Railway is opened (left).
1833 Most German states form a 'common market', ending customs duties.

1824-26 The First Burmese War with Britain.
1825 The Indondesians rebel against the Dutch.
1829 Britain claims Western Australia as part of its empire.
1837 Tokugawa Ieyoshi becomes shogun in Japan. He rules until 1853.

1822 The USA founds Liberia, in West Africa, as a colony for freed slaves.
1824 The first Ashanti war against the British breaks out.
1835 South African Boers leave Cape Colony in the 'Great Trek'.
1836 The Boers defeat the Zulu at the battle of Blood River.

government, but the idea of equal rights for all remained. Just as important was the Industrial Revolution, which changed the lives of millions and created great wealth for some. Both revolutions happened mainly in the West. In 1899 most of Asia and Africa existed under European control.

1840-1859

1840 Upper and Lower Canada are united. They are given self-government in 1841.
1848 The USA gains Texas, New Mexico and California from Mexico.
1848 Gold is discovered in California.
1859 The first US oil well is set up, in Pennsylvania.

1840 Britain introduces the use of postage stamps.
1845 Severe famine affects Ireland.
1848 The 'Year of Revolutions', outbreaks throughout mainland Europe.
1852 The French Second Republic falls.
1854 The Crimean War breaks out.
1857 The Irish Republican Brotherhood is founded to fight for Irish independence from Britain.
1859 Darwin's *Origin of Species* is published in England.

1840 Britain takes over New Zealand with the Treaty of Waitingi.
1842 In the first 'Opium War', Britain takes Hong Kong from China.
c.1845 The British take over the major states in northern India.
1851 The Taiping Rebellion against the Qing breaks out in China.
1854 The USA forces Japan to open its ports to international trade.
1857 Indians rebel against British rule.
1858 China is forced to grant extra rights to foreign nations in the second 'Opium War'.

1843 The British take control of Natal as a colony.
1848 Algeria is declared part of France.
1853-56 Livingstone crosses Africa and reaches the Victoria Falls (right).

1860-1879

1861 The American Civil War breaks out.
1867 The USA buys Alaska from Russia.
1867 Canada becomes a British dominion, with self-government.
1869 The first railway is built across North America.
1876 Alexander Graham Bell invents the telephone.

1861 Italy is united and independent.
1861 Serfdom ends in Russia.
1864 Prussia takes Schleswig-Holstein from Denmark.
1866 Austria is defeated in a war with Prussia.
1867 Hungary gains self-government under the Austrian emperor.
1870 France is defeated in a war with Prussia.
1871 The king of Prussia becomes emperor of Germany.
1871 The French Third Republic begins.
1871 The Revolutionary Commune in Paris is crushed by troops.
1878 The Congress of Berlin establishes some Balkan countries as independent of the Ottoman Empire.

1861 Women gain the right to vote in Australia.
1863 France takes over Indo-China, in south-east Asia.
1865 King Kojong introduces reforms in Korea.
1865 In New Zealand the seat of government moves from Auckland to Wellington.
1868 Rama V comes to the throne in Thailand. He reigns until 1910 and makes many reforms.

1869 The Suez Canal is opened, linking the Red Sea with the Mediterranean.
1870s Samori Turé (right) builds a large trading empire in the upper Niger region.
1879 The Zulus fight the British.
1879 The British gain control of Afghanistan.

1880-1899

1876 At Little Bighorn, Montana, the Sioux defeat US troops led by Lieutenant Colonel Custer. A Sioux bow and arrows (left).
1886 The 'Indian Wars' against Native Americans, end in the USA.

1885 German Karl Benz is the first to sell motor cars.
1889 The Eiffel Tower (right) is built in Paris.
1890 Luxembourg becomes independent from the Netherlands.

1885 The Indian National Congress is founded.
1893 In New Zealand women gain the right to vote.
1894 Korea becomes independent in the war between Japan and China.
1898 The USA gains Puerto Rico and the Philippines in a war against Spain.

1881-98 Most of Africa comes under European colonial rule.
1881 The French take over Tunisia.
1882 The British take over Egypt.
1885 The Congo becomes the personal property of the king of Belgium.
1886 The discovery of gold in the Transvaal leads to the foundation of Johannesburg.
1899 The South African War breaks out, with the Boers fighting the British.

Glossary

mercenary A professional soldier, willing to fight for anyone who pays him.

merchant A person who lives by buying and selling goods. It usually means someone quite rich, more than a simple trader.

militia An armed force. Unlike an army, a militia is a local group of part-time soldiers, who are called up in an emergency, such as a rebellion.

missionary Someone, usually a Christian, who teaches their religion to people of other beliefs.

monastery A community of people (monks) who live according to strict religious rules.

mosque A Muslim place of worship.

mutiny A rebellion by soldiers or sailors.

nationalism Support for the idea of the nation, especially in a nation that is ruled by another power.

naval blockade Stopping the trade and shipping of an enemy by preventing his ships entering or leaving port.

Near East The region around the eastern Mediterranean, sometimes including Egypt and south-east Europe.

oligarchy Government by a small group of people, usually aristocrats.

one-party state A government where all power belongs to a single party.

parliament A government assembly, made up of people elected by the citizens. In modern democratic countries, parliament is often the body that makes the laws.

patriotism A person's love of his or her country.

proclamation An official announcement.

regent Someone who rules on behalf of a monarch, when the monarch is unable to rule, often because he or she is too young.

regime A government. It may mean any kind of government, but is often used for a military government or dictatorship.

republic A state that has no monarch. A republic is usually a democracy, with a president and a parliament elected by the people.

revolution A violent change, usually of government (as in the French Revolution of 1789), in which ordinary people take part. The name is sometimes given to other kinds of rapid change (such as the Industrial Revolution in the 19th century).

seal An instrument with a raised design for making a pattern in wax or clay.

serf A person in the service of a lord, who 'owns' him or her. Serfs were not quite slaves, as they had some rights.

shogun The military governor, or ruler, of Japan from the 12th to 19th centuries.

socialism A form of government in which all the wealth of a country belongs to the people, not private owners.

statesman A politician or government official of great ability, especially one who has an influence on international affairs.

telegraph A method of sending signals by electric wire. Messages are turned into a code, made by signals of different length.

Third Estate The representatives of ordinary, middle-class people who, with the First and Second Estates (nobles and clergy) made up the Estates General in France before the 1789 Revolution.

trade union An organisation to protect the rights of workers.

Index

A

Page numbers in *italic type* refer to illustrations.

Aborigines (Australian) 14, *15*, 24
Afghanistan 41
Africa 7
   European exploration and colonies *34*, 35, 41
   Scramble for 34–35, 41
Afrikaners *35*, 40, 41
Agricultural Revolution *16*
aircraft 38
Alaska 41
Algeria 35, 41
Alsace 33
America *see* United States of America
American Civil War 26–7, 41
American Revolution 8–9, 10
anaesthetics 38, *39*, 40
antseptics 39
aqueducts *18*
Argentina 33
Ashanti *35*
Ashanti Wars 35, 40
Athens 40
Atlanta 27
Aukland 41
Austerlitz, Battle of *12*
Australia 7, *14–15*, 21, 24, 25, 35, 40, 41
   Aborigines 14, *15*, 24
   convict settlements 15
Austria 12, 33
Austrian Empire 33, 41
Austro-Prussian War 41

B

Babbage, Charles 38
Balkans 32, 41
banking 7, 16
Bastille, storming of *11*
Beijing 30
Belgium 32, 40, 41
Bell, Alexander Graham 39, 41
Bengal 28
Benz, Karl 39, 41
Berlin Conference 34
Berlin, Congress of 41
Bessemer, Henry 38
bicycles 38
biology 38
Bismarck, Otto von 33, 42
blast furnaces 17
Blood River, Battle of 40
boats *14*
Boer War *see* South African War
Boers *see* Afrikaners
Bolívar, Simón *33*, 40, *42*
Bolivia 33, 40
Bombay *28–29*
Bonaparte, Napoleon *see* Napoleon I,

French Emperor
boomerangs 15
Boston Tea Party *8*
Boxer Rebellion *30*
Brassey, Thomas 18
Brazil 33
Britain *see* Great Britain
British Empire 7, 30
   Africa 34–35, 40, 41
   Dominions 35, 41
   India *28–29*, 40, 41
   North America 8–9
building *38–39*
Bull Run, Battle of 27
Burke, Robert O'Hara 24
Burmese Wars 40

C

California 36, 41
Cambodia 25, 30
Canada 21, 35, 40, 41
canals 16, *18*, 19
canoes *14*
Cape Colony 35, 40
Cape of Good Hope 35
Carnegie, Andrew *37*
Cavour, Count Camillo di 32, 42
Central America 33
Chakri dynasty 40
Cheyenne 36
child labour *20*, 21
Chile 33
China
   Boxer Rebellion *30*
   Opium Wars 30, 41
   Qing (Manchu) dynasty 41
   republic 30
   Taiping Rebellion 30, 41
   trade 7, 30
cholera 21
Christian missionaries 25, 28, 30, 34
cinema 39
cities and towns *20*, 21
coal 16, 17, 20
Colombia 33
colonies
   European 24–25, *25*
   Scramble for Africa *34*, 35, 41
Common Sense (Paine) 8
communications 19
communism 23
Communist Manifesto (Marx) 23
computers 38
Confederate States *26*, 27
Congo 34, 41
Continental Congress 9
Cook, Captain James *14*
Corvée *10*
cotton 16
crafts 16
Creoles 33

Crimean War 32, 41
Custer, George Armstrong 36, 41

D

Daguerre, Louis 38
Darwin, Charles *38*, 41, 42
Davis, Jefferson 27
decimal system 40
Declaration of Independence 8, *9*, 40
deforestation *37*
Denmark 41

E

East India Companies 8, *28–29*
Ecuador 33
Edison, Thomas *39*
education 23, 38
Egypt 34, 41
Eiffel, Gustave 38
Eiffel Tower (Paris) 38, *41*
electricity 38
energy supply
   coal 16, 17
   fossil fuels 17, *41*
   oil *41*
   steam engines *17*
Essen *33*
Europe
   colonies 24–5, *25*, *34*, 35, 41
   French Revolutionary Wars 40
   independent nations 32–33
   Naopoleonic *12*, 13, 40
   year of revolutions 7, 22, 41
   see also individual countries
evolution, theory of 38
exploration 14, 41

F

factories 16–17, 18, *20–21*
Faraday, Michael 38
farming *16*
films *see* cinema

Index

Index

Acknowledgements

Picture research by Caroline Wood

The publisher would like to thank the following for illustrations:

Chris Brown; p10c, p11r, p15c, p20bl, p21cr, p24b, p30t, p36tr
Tim Clarey; p9t, p10t, p20t, p33t, p42
Gino D'Achille; back cover, p17tr, p18b, p19br, p25t, p29t, p32t, p38-39b, p40-41
Alan Marks; p14br
Steve Noon; p26b, p26tr, p32bl, p35bl
Olive Pearson; all maps
Martin Sanders; p8t

The publisher would like to thank the following for permission to use photographs:

Front cover BAL "Statens Museum For Kunst, Copenhagen, Denmark"; p8b BAL, Private Collection; p9b BAL, "Library of Congress, Washington D.C., USA"; p11tl AKG; p12-13 ET, Musée de Grosbois du Chateau; p13tl Archives Nationales, "Centre Historique des Archives Nationales,Atelier de Photographie,Paris.AE/I/23(no 10 et 12/1)"; p13tr ET , "Musée de L'Armee, Paris"; p14t Bishop Museum; p15t Robert Harding, Robert Francis; p16b ET, Lincoln Museum & Art Galleries(detail); p17bl Science & Society Picture Library, Science Museum; p18t Collections, Ed Gabriel; p19t ET, National Maritime Museum; p20-21t Corbis, Library of Congress; p21bl ET, Domenica del Corriere; p22b AKG, "Kunstmuseum, Dusseldorf"; p23t BAL, Towner Art Gallery; p23cr BAL, "Private Collection,The Stapleton Collection"; p24tr BAL, "National Library of Australia,Canberra,Australia"; p26-27t AKG,; p27br AKG,; p28t BAL, "British Library,London,UK"; p28-29 Corbis, Arvind Garg; p29b By permission of The British Library IOL.T 10951; p30c AKG; p31t Werner Forman Archive, BM; p31 BM; p33br Mary Evans Picture Library; p34bl Jean-Loup Charmet; p35br Mary Evans Picture Library; p36bl BAL, "D.F.Barry,Bismarck,Dakota"; p37tr Corbis, Bettmann; p38-391 Collections, Brian Shuel; p39cr Corbis, Hulton-Deutsch Collection

Key: BAL = Bridgeman Art Library; BM = The British Museum; V&A = Victoria & Albert Museum; ET = E.T. Archive; SPL = Science Photo Library;
    AKG = AKG London; MH = Michael Holford